WORD-MADE WORLD

Also by Chee Brossy:

The Strings Are Lightning and Hold You In

Burntwater

Fighters

WORD-MADE WORLD

Chee Brossy

WINNER OF THE 2024 WASHINGTON PRIZE

Andrea Carter Brown
Series Editor

Word-Made World © 2025 Chee Brossy

Reproduction
of this book in any form
or by any means, electronic or
mechanical, except when quoted
in part for purpose of review,
must be with permission
in writing from the
publisher.

Address inquiries to
THE WORD WORKS
P. O. Box 42164
Washington, DC 20015
editor@wordworksbooks.org

No part of this book may be used
or reproduced in any manner
for the purpose of training
artificial intelligence
technologies
or systems.
Ever.

Cover Design by Susan Pearce
Cover Photograph by Chee Brossy
Author Photograph by Teresa Montoya

ISBN 978-1-944585-88-4

Acknowledgments

I am deeply grateful to:

My mother Mariana and father Peter, áádóó bił háíjéé' shínaaí Jackson dóó shideezhí Stacy for being my family and showing me support that cannot be described in words. My late grandmother Annie who taught me strength. My late grandfather Chester, shicheii nít'éé', who taught me spirit and nobility. My friend Jon for editing, for the many conversations about writing and poetry. I am grateful for Diné Bikéyah and the land and water that we call home. Éí baa ahééh nisin. I am grateful to Andrea and the team at The Word Works for believing in this manuscript and bringing it all together.

My acknowledgment to the editors of the following publications in which these poems first appeared:

> *Conduit*: "Female Rain"
> *Southern Indiana Review*: "Offering"
> *Tampa Review*: "Inverted Weaving"

Contents

Dikos / The Year of Loss . . . 3
Offering . . . 5
Inverted Weaving . . . 6
Fourth Person . . . 7
Unfêted . . . 8
Ochre-Orange for Evening Sky . . . 9
Níyá . . . 10
Pueblo Bread and Gravitron . . . 11
Bá'ólta'í / For Whom One Reads . . . 12
Female Rain . . . 13
Word-Made World . . . 14
Burn . . . 17
Sounding the Cave . . . 18
Azhá Shíí . . . 19
Zozobra, Man of Gloom . . . 20
The Polishing That Brings Understanding . . . 21
Carrying the Theory Forward . . . 22
Staggering Deer and Technician with Grinder . . . 24
Shepherd's Turnaround . . . 25
Weathervane . . . 26
After Gas and Dust and Gravity . . . 27
All-Caps . . . 28
Not Enough . . . 30
Helper . . . 32
Shalako . . . 33
Hashtł'ish . . . 35
Hiking the Gorge . . . 37
K'ad Éí Ahił Hwiilne' Dooleeł . . . 39
The Sun's Journey Across the Sky . . . 40
Autumn in New England . . . 42
Shield . . . 43
Sacred Mountains . . . 45
Aak'ee / Fall . . . 46
The Warning . . . 48
North / Náhookos . . . 50
Why It's Like This . . . 52
Handmade . . . 53
The Killing Grass . . . 54

University . . . 55
Nomenclature . . . 57
Creation Story . . . 58
A Wedding . . . 60
Dididooljah . . . 61
A Speech . . . 63
Swifts and Swallows . . . 64
Counting . . . 66
Warlike . . . 67
Neighborhood . . . 68
Work . . . 70
Adolescence . . . 71
Idiom . . . 72

About the Author . . . 75
About The Word Works . . . 76
Washington Prize Winners . . . 77

For my family

Dikos / The Year of Loss

In the month of July, of Heavy Sowing,
seeds heat-rising, tendrils wet-seeking,
the infant corn started in cardboard cups
grows initially green, fat, moisture-rich.

Then, forgotten for days on the car's flaking roof,
the plants wilt, dry, and yellow.
The monsoons arrive in the afternoons, too late.
And so love ends.

The moon of Small Ripening, Initial Ripening,
arrives and with it mosquitos and biting flies,
with it a beginning that must be excavated
from the mind's drying dirt.

Plastic irrigation lines dehydrate,
brittle like hair loosed from the scalp.
Year's end will arrive next month
at the conclusion of Full-Grown Ripening,
the denouement of the third and final
quartet of the year.

Yet we are still secluded in our houses
and apartments when September arrives.
Masked, we twist away from a stranger's breath,
grunt, give curt nods and waves,
infectious in our misanthropy.

And so we come to *Ghaajį'*,
Backbone, and summit the cordillera,
the ridge frosted with young snow,
a youthful chill wafting, blowing,
now gusting our faces.

On the other side: fat bears prepare caves,
leaves yellow, and this year the cold
will excise the aspen sack-worms
from the viewing scopes atop the ridge,

and restore a green, glittering glow.
The year is new, winter coming,
the Gods emerging,
our breath clouding as we sing.

But perhaps this is too hopeful,
assuming too much. It is only natural
within nature, only customary within custom,
only hereditary within the cultivated.
Webs and cocoons still mar our sight.

We must reach January's Melting Freeze—
when the sun melts the top layer of snow
only for it to freeze again each night—
with our lungs still intact,

in order to witness Eaglets Hatching,
then hear their First Worried Calls,
to measure the Growth of Small Wings,
and praise the Explosion of Flight.

Offering

Ash is the standard mode of protection,
future tense in the prefix, action in the suffix—
the most crucial element saved for last,
a natural drama and hierarchy, from man
to horse, to ponderosa, to grass, to sandstone.

My hands sting today after a fall on a mountain trail.
Skin peels easily, infects easily, secretes naturally—
a distraction, like a friend who visits and takes you
for a night out, a brief forgetting of ailments.

But it is we who must apologize,
return to the earth and make an offering
for striking her with our body—
Shimá, of course, means Mother.

There was a bird in the yard this morning,
too young and small to fly.
Flapping, stumbling, stuttering wings.
Other birds flew down in turns,
hopping beside it, then flying a short way

to alight again on the gravel, chirping,
then flying back up into the plum tree.
They were a team saying,
See, this is the way, little stammer.

Clean thoroughly, apply ointment,
bandage, deposit wrappings in the trash.
As a mother says to her son
when the bullies have had him,

when he struggles to raise his head,
My beautiful son, my precious, precious boy.

Inverted Weaving

The stirring sticks grow heavy when cooking blue corn mush,
caked as shoes in mud. Palms blister as you bend to work.
The top layer solidifies, collecting a callous love.

A hydrogen peroxide shortage so we bathe in bleach,
rinse our hair with isopropyl alcohol, and drink iodine for a lucid X-ray.

The verb is shínítbéézh, *you* boiled it, past tense, completed the course,
stayed in the hospital five full days, accepted the medication intravenously
along with shame, judgment, pity.

A party in the wealthy north side of Santa Fe has been shattered by gunshots
Eighteen, lithe and long-limbed, our star player lies bleeding on the concrete
We watch as if it were a summer blockbuster of the kind we've been deprived

The papers cover the throngs, the vigils, the funeral, the tournaments
        in his name.
Eventually, the dedication of a basketball court. They say, *If only the gyms
were still open, the youth centers, the swimming pools, he might still be alive.*

The summer sun sinks to the horizon where it waits, held up by the skyline,
allowing us the anticipated beauty, the inverted weaving.
On this day it drifted away from us, taking a life.

Tomorrow, may the sun be on your side.

Fourth Person

Blue masks lie crumpled in the supermarket parking lot,
soiled with tire marks, discarded as though their wearers were fleeing.
Recalling other times, epochs of fear and retreat,
choosing which horses to ride and which to sacrifice.

But always, too, the outstretched hand to grasp, lift, embrace.
Some even discovered breath after a morning's eastward run
filled their lungs. Where before it took all your strength
to remain intact as you knelt and clutched the Earth.

Now, again, we suffer loss. Many slip away and we must imagine
the mint-green curtain, the noise of breathing machines,
the bedpans and corrugated tubes because we cannot sit corporeal
in the hospital room for their comfort or ours,

and instead begin mourning first in our tattered dreams,
in our minds of ribboned memory, freighted as we are with solidity.
We remember that teachings are said in the fourth person:
K'éédazhdidléehgo, nazhniłkaadgo, tádazhdigéeshgo, hadazhniłchaadgo.

Similarly, fourth person describes a past:
One planted, farmed, herded, sheared, washed,
carded, spun, wove. Taught, spoke, walked, rode.
When one learns and lives concurrently, there is no distance—

the past lives among us, the will of others courses through.
A stream weaves between rocks, monsoons accompany thunder,
and irrigation fills the dry furrows.

Unfêted

Does the weaving begin with the weft, warp, and loom,
with batten and comb, the muffled, tamping thud—
or the washing, carding, and spinning of wool?

With the herding of sheep, the mapping of springs,
streams, creeks, and pools of water? Or freedom
after long imprisonment, starvation, illness,

the death of one's children? After sacrificing the body
for a handful of chalky, plastery flour?
Brilliant blues, streaked indigo, sunset-orange,

cochineal-red. Whether pictorial, figural,
corn-stalked, arrow-borne, or layered simply:
white, red, blue, black—chief blankets.

To have squeezed one's veins of skill and poured
such pain and joy into a work of art as to transform it
into a bridge to another world.

This month's art display on the coffee shop's walls
is in honor of the August Indian Market,
which has gone uncrowded, unfestivaled,

unfêted this year, the country still in the throes
of disease and disorder. The artists are absent,
the weavings completed circa 1890-1905 or 1911-1915,

property of the Shop Down the Street;
these artists were not here last year, either.
But the pang is always a surprise, the jolt sudden

and electric. One can reach out and touch the bow,
the arrow. Feel the weave—still tight.
Up close the wool is rough, uneven, bristling with life.

Ochre-Orange for Evening Sky

One lifetime of learning is what we're allotted.
How many languages do you choose? How many love affairs?

How many are chosen for you? Does understanding strike
when you have thick, lustrous hair, or after you've shorn it close?

A shearing that, post-radiation, never regrows, spring after spring,
straining to remember a prayer's ending, how to mix ochre-orange

for evening sky, the canvas propped unfinished on the easel,
the people, trees, and receding mountains still ghosts in graphite.

They say our hair are our thoughts—tie them neatly, securely,
or yishbizhgo, braid them, and if they fall out,

retrieve them to be added back for fullness—or burned.
For harm resides all around, awaiting the next slip,

the stumble on loose shale, your full weight landing
on a quicker player's instep, the crack reverberating

up your femur into your jaw, provided you are not careful.

Níyá

Our minds will fade before our bodies,
before anatomy and beating artery.

Níyá means "I have arrived"
or, "he has arrived."

Through the screen we decipher furrows
and half-smiles—is that coughing or laughter?

If there is good to be photosynthesized
out of this smoke we call chlorophyll,
out of the noise we call carbon dioxide,
there is no use waiting.
Man-made material persists in the ocean,
diffusing throughout, not only the surface.

Our squabbling, wailing, and feasting
have shaken humanity into opposing poles.

Áádéé' níyá—I have arrived
from the East Pathway.

What angers you so?
The birds shitting on your car?
The belching trucks speeding through your neighborhood?

Retrieve your broom, knock them from their nest.
Put up a sign: Children at Play.

Pigeons hoot accusingly from the telephone pole,
while men agitate, gesticulate behind their steering wheels.

Pueblo Bread and Gravitron

The faint, dead taste of mold in the Pueblo oven bread
forgotten a day too long in the cupboard
turning beneath raspberry jam.

Towering House, an original clan,
refers possibly to a Pueblo origin.
White is its color.

Today they bring teachers back into dusty school halls,
into classrooms with two high windows each,
sealed, no ventilation.

Return from your hiatus, People,
from the poles you've staked.

From the walls of the Gravitron
where, pressed flat by centrifugal force,
you've been screaming.

What does it matter now who flung the switch—
the baked, skeletal carnie
or one of you in this sweat-dampened darkness?

All I know: the wind waits outside fresh
and dry, waving in the summer forest fires,
a diffuse and sweeping sunrise.

Bá'ólta'í / For Whom One Reads

Our language teacher juts her lips back and forth
around her teeth while blowing air under her tongue
to demonstrate the aspirant L,
the voiceless L, the Navajo L

so we will be unembarrassed by our own spittle,
sprouting as it does among the mannerly,
muted English consonants.

Gone now, she's the one who taught us
that the fourth person is holy—
pay attention when the elderly employ it,

assume a straight back when you conjugate yourself.
We laughed at her and with her,
and honored her with our saliva.

Female Rain

Red ants swarm the lizard carcass,
desiccating, removing what glistens,
chewing with a collective, tireless jaw.

The skunk also is roadkill, its lacerated glands seeping musk,
radiating the sidewalk so one must cross the street.

Two nights ago the moon was three quarters full—
but I couldn't say if it was growing or darkening.

The pregnancy test strangely charged
as it sits unopened on the table.

Patchouli emanates from our neighbors across the street,
while next door, visitors have arrived

in a tall, country-crossing van complete with stove,
beds, curtains, a young, mustachioed man,
an exuberant, tank-topping woman.

Finally, summer's fever has broken,
the weeks of sweaty record heat speared
these two days by clouds and rain—

first, thundering male,
complete with horizontal lightning,

then female this morning, playing on my face,
sounding a papery patter on my surgical mask.

Reminding me of the twinning of oneself,
of one's legs, the left hand, and the right.

Word-Made World

The boundaries are crisp like a rooster's scorching call
at five a.m. through a window's futile breeze-beckon,
amid a fire-scaled summer, our morals in high relief,
at least in our minds, in our ephemeral word-made worlds.

The rooster has kicked up the hens' squawking,
the honking geese, the gobbling turkeys,
finally the howling of two sad-faced mutts, one large
and lumbering, the other dark and compact.

The burn climbs up the mountain alongside scars
from years past scorching thousands of acres,
threatening the ski basin—twenty five percent contained,
five percent tomorrow, none the day after.

Near enough to taste the smoke that drifts
into our dreams in the REM-dead of each night,
that mixes with the funk of the neighborhood skunks,
creating weeks of daytime fog,

emulating our bloated thoughts as they stack
above our heads, teeter without liberation
in our isolation, the radical becoming normal,

extremism quotidian, violence the only release
in our narrow-necked bottles, translucent vessels

of our own construction.

≈

At night the men come and go, the walls of their adobe house
crumbling, a white construction permit affixed permanently
to a window lit by fluorescent light.

Through the door, open on summer nights,
I see them sitting around a table, cards in hand, smoking,
exclaiming, *Ay, Güey!* and throwing them down.
The roosters, hens, geese, turkeys, dogs are theirs.

Sometimes at dusk a woman parks her blue Toyota
and in hushed tones talks with one of the men.
I can't tell if this is courtship or hardship or family.
They have been there around the corner
for as long as I, but never a conversation between us.

Next door, a church—
spot-lit spire rising, parishioners cautiously returning.
Now the parking lot grows full on Sunday,
on Saturday a small, masked wedding,
Wednesday a funeral of "Taps" and cowboy hats.

O sages, O ancestors, O matriarchs,
the mornings, come early,
find us lying crosswise in our beds,
sheets pulled over our eyes,
awaiting your yanking back of the curtains,
your splash of water to the face,
your scolding yell wrenching us dayward,
straightening, setting us in place.

≈

Perhaps they are Mayan, or Achí de Guatemala
and survived a torturous trek through the Sonoran desert,

crossed on O'odham land where once
a grandmother would have left a pump handle up,

to signal it was okay to cross, to drink her water.
Before federal policies narrowed and funneled,

cut families down the middle—
the Kickapoo, whose land was severed by the border,

whose Mexican-side healers still practice
where Spanish is the lingua Franca—

when migrants could still be people.
Now many more die crossing, and even the tribal police

are inured to the regular desiccation, the strange lightness
of a human body after days, weeks, months in the sun.

Burn

With its harsh words, its dangerous
and indiscriminate fire, protection is male.
K'é—family and its interlocking network,
a matrix of care and reciprocity—female.

Way of shield and arrow, spear, defense, aggression
mixed within us, fluctuating over the years,
rising to froth the surface when unsettled,

and once released, difficult to put away.
Anger when a dog barks out a truck window
into your ear, when drivers stare too long at you

on the sidewalk and shout insults under the cover of night—
a blaze of brake lights,
fists, crowbar, baseball bat, gun—

the ease of the switch something I have realized late
or early depending on the judge, perhaps in black robes,
sometimes clothed in a loved one.

Our fathers are many, biological first if we are lucky,
then his brothers, provided they come around,
then his clan brothers extended.

Or perhaps your father was absent
and you were shown the rites by maternal uncles.
Always, of course, the Sun.

The first light you see every morning, if you have won
comprehension, if you understand that fire can feel cold,
numbing, just as ice can burn and set your skin aflame.

Sounding the Cave

The eating of fish, the night whistle,
meeting face-to-face with one's mother-in-law,
death coming haphazardly into a conversation,
inviting one's own misfortune or a loved one's.
Therefore, to prepare the ceremonial payment,
fold the blanket just so.

In a canyon one shouts and hears the response echoed,
bouncing off the stone walls, indicating a full,
sound structure. The walls of our cheeks,
our poised tongues, dams of teeth,
abundance and viscosity of saliva.

The wind in our lungs gives meaning
to the morning run, exclamation and exhalation
priming our instruments, sounding the cave
for the day's battles, the wars we fight.

For one must show oneself worthy,
trained properly, muscles taxed and toned.
The alternative is to be without spirit,
a listless spine draped over the sofa,
the blue-lit screen, staring.
Waiting for the day to start
instead of rising, greeting the sun.

Azhá Shíí

Shoulder-length hair disheveled,
greasy shirt buttoned askew,
face dark and sun-weathered,
dirty jeans, beat-up basketball shoes,
ch'ízhii hands stuffed in pockets—
the drunk who accosted you
in the supermarket parking lot,
blinking slowly, swaying a bit.
He'd asked for money, a ride to Crystal.
Come on, brother, show some
love for a guy down on his luck.
In response to your disdain,
your shooing rejection,
your accusation, in Navajo,
that he is a no-good, sorry
disgrace to the Navajo people—
who taught him to act like this
anyway? he switched to Navajo himself.

Azhá shíí ndi, that may be so, and yet,
according to K'é, the laws that govern
our society, our people, I am still
your relative, your brother,
your son, your maternal uncle,
your little father. Who are you
to shoo me away? You haughty,
small man in a big suit,
truck that's too giant for your small self.
I asked nicely, and here you insult me,
your own clan, your own blood,
your own people. You can go to hell.

He turned on his heel, nearly falling,
swiped his hand heedlessly, violently,
swiping you away, erasing you,
and shook his head, cursing you
and your fine boots, your clean shirt,
the impossibly shiny horse you rode in on.

Zozobra, Man of Gloom

Pigeons roost in the paper birch,
smoke fills the eastern air and seeps westward,
diffusing into the permeable soul
as water permeates skin,
as alcohol enters the stomach lining.

One day an egg falls from the tree
and splatters onto the gravel driveway.
The tenant also finds spatters of yolk
on the spoiler of his white car,
then knocks the nest off with a broom
to end the shower of droppings.

The summer was measured
in stifling, sweaty afternoons—
how many could stack onto each other,
like newspapers in a recycling bin,
insults filed in the cabinet of memory,
each tab scribed neatly
in capitalized title case.

The effigy burned last night
vested in a white robe-dress
of Éé' Neeshoodii style—
Jesuit, One-Whose-Clothes-Drag—
lips cartoonishly large and red,
eyes sunken and shadowed,
moaning, groaning, then screaming,
waving his robotic arms,
now enveloped in flames
taller than the new Big Box façade.

Everything is fine, he said at first.
What disaster? I see no smoke.
Your mind plays tricks, deceives your eyes.
The windows of your house
are not shaking, flames do not lick
the paintings on the walls.

The Polishing That Brings Understanding

To stand straight, back strong,
the male turquoise hanging from your ears,
the white shell beads female around your neck,
at your wrist silver—the evidence of your effort,
and prowess, the wrestling, bending,
hammering, filing, grinding, sanding,
chemicalizing, oxidizing, acid etching
and finally polishing that brings understanding.

When you stand there vested in these hard-won
insights, then may you reach to past selves,
brush their clothes of dirt and mud,
lick your finger to blot the blood at their collar,
wipe dried saliva from their cheek, straighten
a spine with your hands on their shoulders.

The brilliant depths of the blue reminding you,
the wet click of the strands against your chest.
Then turn and cast a plan forward
like a net, a textile of dreams,
layer the words so you straighten, rise,
stand on them as they gird the skeleton with muscle,
sinew, tendons, veins, blood, air.

For today has arrived cool, the weather changing
as all things change. The wind hints
at midday gusts; crows rise over
the mountain ridge on thermals barking,
unrestrained, mirthful harbingers of change.

Carrying the Theory Forward

What face behind your mask?
what frowns hiding?
what smile lines—silent arcs
curved toward each other

like a cowboy's hooked legs,
green plastic chaps,
missing its toy horse?

A hummingbird descends on the tree
of red, leafy flowers, living in luxury.

The atom bomb has been discovered
by bounding, disheveled men,
ecstatic, in a lab in Los Alamos.

But four years later, still no accurate
theory for quantum mechanics
when wave after wave of B-29s

lay waste to low-lying Tokyo,
and now we have modern, corporate physics.
Carrying the theory forward:

No one word matters more than another.
There is no hierarchy of words,
no one event freighted more than another.
Indifference is the driving force,

the framework of all life.
Lightning strikes, forest fires,
car crashes, genocide, state violence,
state garrote meted out arbitrarily—
casual, wanton, motiveless—

This then is the rule? The theorem.
The evidence, empirical.
But momentary: a tight-framed cinema,

black bars obscuring the peripheries;
we see only loved ones drowning,
forced to ford the Rio Grande.

Tight shot of a train's whistle,
a scream as it steams.
No one word is above any other:

everything is happening at once.
There are multiples of you.
The structure of crystal is plastic

as mountains are plastic over time,
as Mauna Loa and Mauna Kea are young,
their ridges grassy but sharp,

some mountains male, steeply climbing,
others female, welcoming,
encouraging divergent thoughts

and meditations as you sweat your gyre.
At the top is a view: the range rolls to the east,
the town arrayed in the valley below,

highways glint with trucks—
silent, distant, awaiting your return.

Staggering Deer and Technician with Grinder

The disjointed lurch through uncertainty and peril
that fogs our glasses with each breath in the newfound
cold like the deer's stagger through woods,
pierced in the haunch by an arrow, willing itself on,
no longer straining to hear the hunter—
crunch of snow, twig, or crisp leaf.

The permit tags are plentiful this year
and whole lineages of men—grandfather, father,
son, uncle, nephew—call in sick.

The sculptor's technician steps back from her work
on the model, the grinder in her hand slowing its whir,
imagines the angles and joints, curvilinear whirl of steel
scaled at nine, tall as a wave double overhead,
finished with a red patina, anchored obscurely
onto a spinning travertine base.

The sculptor can no longer grind for nerve damage
in his dominant arm. A champion, a show-winner,
this wind-inspired whirl.

Our startle has saved us the quick and certain death,
setting in motion a vast but unconnected array of professions
and we remind ourselves what it means to be agent
in one's own life, to build a dike and direct water
to parched corn, to teach a child to say,
I walk forward with pollen at my feet.

Shepherd's Turnaround

The pesticides lie heavy on the strawberries,
the layers of chemicals waxy-smooth on apple skins.
We label our produce organic, health-driven,
special. Having let fall kindness,
where does the spirit find sustenance?
Having erased all the pencil markings
of sun's silhouette on the house walls,
how will we know solstice?
How will we recognize the shepherd's turnaround
when clouds obscure our shadow in early afternoon?

We will drift further and further
from home's corral, no longer marching
but wandering, anxiety filling the hours
like a power plant's haze snaking
the valley floor, climbing the mesa face.
The markings would show us *middle*—
a moment to live by. But blue light flickers
out our windows deep into night,
and we dive into the bar's heavy air.

The wild plums hang from their branches
wrinkling, still yellow, trying to turn orange,
red, purple. But the rainfall has been spare
this summer, so they remain sour
until an early storm leaps down
from the Rockies and freezes them.

Who will light your fire, spirit?
The fire poke hangs above the door
dormant, unfamiliar now with ember
and ash. Your path is unclear, missing
the bright yellow paint, the silver reflectors.
But the bowl that holds these colors
is on your bedside table, awaiting excavation.
Show me what it means to make warmth.
What it means to say *cold*.

Weathervane

Fog arrives in the night, steaming until we are soaked.
Morning's light diffuse and cold, but the clouds

envelop us—the gods have descended the foothills,
and stream through the silent streets,

before landscaping trucks prickling with rakes and shovels
slice through, before SUVs barrel and tunnel the swirl.

Stiff shoes wear blisters into heels, the postwoman speaks
loudly into her earpiece a story of indignation and woe.

The green copper weathervane has been removed
from the high clock tower, singled out after all these years

as an outdated diorama—the feathered Indian playing a flute
or pipe, at the feet of the gesticulating patriot,

a barrel of rum under the tall, framing pine.
The alumni magazine says it weighed 600 pounds.

But it seemed so small, trembling in New England's vagaries
as we trudged through snow, or clutched raincoats

about our shoulders on our way to the library.
I was amazed when my friends told me sophomore year.

That's an Indian? I said. No. How strange, how quaint,
the history our enthicketed college prides itself on.

This cloudy weather reminds me of that landscape—
perpetually overcast, green growth, trees threatening

to take back the sleepy-eyed brick buildings, thankful
when the sun breaks through the canopy as it does this morning.

But here we give thanks for the fog and rain, the snow,
the moisture slaking our prolonged summer thirsts.

After Gas and Dust and Gravity

The TV's radiating stare, its vibrations,
the imperceptible tremors that nevertheless
trouble our groggy sleep, causing our shoulders
and backs to ache, like the snap of a rug,
the dust taking so long to fall.

We are the fly that cannot escape,
trapped between a window and venetian blinds,
the way camouflaged to our thousand eyes.
Beyond, the sun shines, reflecting off car hoods
and weeds grow.

It is difficult to rearrange your mind
when the People are drawn as squatting and shirtless,
passive spectators halting their fish-smoke on the beach
when a giant, three-masted ship drops anchor offshore.

If you say it enough, if your repetition is dogged,
your goal of turning fiction into fact clearly defined,
why are we astonished when whole swaths of humanity
follow the enraged, unhinged, trembling leader?
Is it because the goal is so arbitrary?
That there must be reason at least,
behind his relentless pursuit of tumult and turmoil?

The tribe *was* likely shirtless, *did* squat to perform work,
gut fish, prepare the meat, share story and laughter,
and sometimes, yes, just sit. They did travel water
by canoe and paddle and perhaps some form
of this momentous collision was inevitable since the beginning
of human life, of all life, of gas and dust and gravity.

But if so, it was also in myth, in story, in human song
and language—and these exist in the mind,
in the saliva, in the mouth, in the web of thought,
spirit and philosophy that have made the incalculable journey
to arrive at today, at our keyboards, in our sweat-glistened fingertips.

All-Caps

Unraveling each day, the news is a tailless lizard
scurrying on the path in front of us,

scrambling furtively, darting, distracting us
from diverting our eyes to more fruitful pursuits.

Who stepped on it? What cat toyed with it
to cause it to amputate its own tail?

Every day we slip more easily into this carnival,
seek out its hitching scramble,

measuring our hours by the intensity
of its frenzy, breathing just a bit shallower

with every all-caps headline across the front
page of our *trusted online news source.*

Soon we will require herculean font size,
virtually nude lettering to match the inflamed,

fleshy, oil-slicked photographs.
Now, says the editor, *gasoline now!*

We've baited our way to the precipice,
the audience is gorged and turning sluggish,

our darting no longer entices the paw.
We must have shinier lizards, more muscular,

iridescent showmen and women
whose tails grow back in twenty-four hours

longer, twitchier, resplendent with color.
The people chew on the gristle, spit out

the bones, hungry for more.
Somehow all that neon-green and orange

tastes bitter, leaves a stomach roiled and sickly,
needing something to settle it,

so we can keep everything down.

Not Enough

Will we look back and say, *That year was a bad one,
the corn didn't grow and neither did the children?*
Our culture teacher died, leaving a vacuum no one

can replace. Grandfather, too, who'd long outlived
his wife, annoyed even with his nurses at final intake triage,
speaking angrily to them in Navajo, not happy

with all their needles, their oxygenated tubes.
We have renounced the Navajo religion and embraced
the baroque columns of Catholicism.

You chafed at our pitiful standing in the world,
forgotten among the heroes of the country, disgraced
and booted from restaurants, spit on in the parking lots

of shopping malls, rolled and beaten into bloody meat
in some bar alleyway on the edge of streetlight's halo,
under the cold vibration of Main Street's neon signs.

But we are here for you, we say, at home
among the mesas and cottonwood-hung streams,
ready to track down the medicine man the moment

you ask. *Not enough*, you say, not after I've
seen the world, the machined, industrious, broad
streets of sculptured France and Italy,

the bright, inviting lipstick of Germany.
Not to mention—never—death and atrocity.
It takes skill to stay on the edge of remembrance,

to be the living face of loss yet to never give it words.
So we leave you to it, living your entire life in your mind.
If we open the refrigerator and the meat has spoiled,

we must replace the machine for it has broken.
But if instead we pull the crisper and the lettuce has frozen,
then we merely dial back the knob's intensity—

unless it is a sign of the refrigerator's demise,
the exponentially decreasing half-life of the appliance
splitting and splitting again, until all that's left

is a flat hum, a careening, droning silence.
And finally we see you in a wheelchair, back home
at a big gathering, hungering for a microphone.

Yes, we agree, the old ways are gone, never to return,
but whose old ways have you renounced really,
after your myriad travels, ours, or yours?

Helper

Sweep the dirt floor, scoop the vomit—
you must perform the helper's duty without revulsion,
carry out the commonplace, tap the embers onto the shovel,
enkindle the corncob lighter
that we may have smoke, thought, prayer.

After tension and turmoil come reflection and calm;
To carry rage like a razor in your mouth is untenable.
Anger corrodes like hydrochloric acid, burning
without flame, injuring internally so that from without
we appear unscathed, save for our faces—

mouth droop here, eye twitch there,
a general numbness encroaching.
We walk upright, albeit hunched slightly, swing our arms—
from a distance making the figure of a man,
yet one who is strangely hollow, as though in danger

of blowing away at the slightest gust,
of tumbling down the sidewalk in the wake of a garbage truck.
Come now, figure, away from that gaping window.
You must shut them tight, flip the locks closed
when you leave the house—enemies in the neighborhood.

Lock all the doors, knobs, and bolts
and check by hand; only then will your mind
sit right. For the mind must be unfettered by anxiety,
unencumbered by the daily fears, unoccupied
by the ill wills of other spirits

in order to be the helper, to light the tobacco,
to lend your voice to song, and sweep away the oily refuse.

Shalako

Let us examine these fires—the ones that bequeath
smoke to our skies, cast our sunsets in orange

and our mornings in hazy yellow—drifted to us
from western California until the pitched Sandias

are shrouded, the ranging Jemez and pointed Sangre de Cristo
obscured in turn, and we must trust their shadows

will appear as we drive the interstate. From above,
a brown cloud spreads west, ever more dense,

contrasting with the blues, tans, and whites, the valleys
and long plains of the Colorado Plateau, here and there a strip of green.

The Rio Grande, San Juan, and Animas snake through
where forests had been low, ponderosas sparse,

spices hard to come by, salt a precious commodity
that must be traded for with Zunis.

The Shalako carving is bright blue and red, turquoise,
pink, yellow; its blanket made of feathers and clouds.

The artist at my door was hard-up and I gave him the mix
of ones and small bills in my wallet, proud of my purchase for cheap.

Now I see the painstaking hours, the craftsmanship
required to carve its fine hair, paint its mask

and sun-face, burn dark its feathers.
Now I see the fullness of his days, the pride that rich work

brings to life, his wealth in those arenas, though, yes,
he probably used the money for drink or drugs

and still comes around, though I've moved away,
looking for what counts as a reliable customer.

The juniper-carved figure is still bright, neon greens vibrant, its lean still regal, even when turned away.

Hashtł'ish

When a poet goes on about the endless toil of farming
in a small farming town, the work that beats the farmers down
until they spend all their time, even weekday afternoons,

in their cups. Or how he laments the great expanse
of valleys and deserts, hills and mountains, the sheer
monotony of it all, the indifference to the individual,

when he says the land is "unforgiving," that it does not
offer up its bounties willingly like a Greek goddess
of fertility. There is no connection there.

The mountains don't carry stories, don't live
with beings, gods, medicine, specific strengths
and dangers, attributes not found in the peaks and ridges

seventy miles to the east, who don't carry their own wisdoms.
The waters, rivers, lakes, don't carry knowledge
of a clan's foundation, of its responsibilities.

Everything is impersonal, only "what a man makes
with his own two hands." But the only vacuum
is in the mind, the only nullius in the spirit.

No wonder then, the machinations of philosophy,
the artifice of government—to build a lattice
on a swamp, to lay foundation in a mire.

No wonder we mistakenly look to the loudest,
most frenzied mouths and minds to correct us,
to jolt us out of ignorance, believing this brief thrill

of self-flagellation will sustain us beyond its flare,
believing in their professed wisdom, the fakes
who call themselves sage, who brandish their torches

as if they were the fires of knowledge.
Who then, should we follow? The language teacher
who stagnates, teaching the same simple days of the week,

numbers on a clock, joking with students already fluent?
No, there must be work, the slow work
of understanding, of putting words to our morass,

hashtł'ish being *mud*, one driver pushing,
the other reining the horses, realigning
the wheels for the best passage onto drier ground.

Hiking the Gorge

On the mountain, piñon trees have begun
to release their nuts in preparation for the new year.
Gum that glistened in summer turns opaque as the cones open.
Assistance, Little Grandfather, is what we ask for.
The earth is feverish, burning orange, filling the sky
with carbon residue, mirroring our own rising temperatures,
frustrations and angers, long-buried traumas
emerging, banging loudly on the sides of our heads.

Hold two meanings in your mind—
evolution and the Holy Beings,
the sobering depths, festering wounds of history,
and the joy in applying the enemy's language.
A wave and a particle, fierce protection of a child,
knowing you would protect them with deadly violence,
and still push them out of the nest, and calculate
when the bully was their own obstacle.
A teenage party where drink certainly, drugs possibly,
sex, too, and yes, the potential that a feud will escalate
to fists, to a sixteen-year-old pulling a gun
and firing it into your child's chest.

Perhaps we can protect them during the years of high school,
but someday soon the jaws of calamity will snap shut
and then it is chance whether they survive
intact, grow, able again to smile at the day—
or with a darkened face, crushed forever.

Then we will know if our preparation was enough—
the infrequent runs at dawn, the sporadic visits
to grandparents and extended family.
But one cannot win, either, by kicking the child out,
expecting them to learn the world, to swim the swollen,
churning Rio Grande without instruction.

In the streams live the Gods, in the morning's streaking rise,
in our faces reflected back to us in a canyon pool,
in the warmth gathering in black lava rocks that line the trail
as we ascend to our assorted lives, jobs, and families.

Water relieves us of our fears, streams them from us,
as it does starch from rice, the everyday chaff.
Let us sing with the sweat of our bodies, our labored breath.
Crest the rim of the gorge, look back upon the green shock below.

K'ad Éí Ahił Hwiilne' Dooleeł

To have it smoldering always, that fire,
to defend ourselves and our loved ones,
inflaming us that we might pack our belongings,
set one child on the motorcycle seat in front of us,
the other behind, wife holding tight,
bags hanging from handlebars, and leave our village
as smoke billows across the sky and soldiers march
through our suddenly unfamiliar streets.

Such is the role of fire.
But turning it off is another matter.
Not as easy as turning down the gas burner
on a kitchen stove, as kicking dirt on a campfire—
because these fires burn *within*, háni', the body, the self.

In a grease fire, throwing water can cause flames to jump
and engulf others. You might try distracting the fire,
feeding it small morsels, chips of wood, clumps of grass,
tin bean and meat cans to watch the papering
curl and smoke. But this does nothing to ease it,
only adds a chemical hue to the flames.

No, it is a long and taxing process, calming the fire.
Perhaps the work of lifetimes. Because what is calm
when danger lurks behind smiling faces, even when
the people are working and the goods are cheap?
That is what it means to say *harmony*, to say *balance*,
to say *equilibrium* has been reached.

The old newspaper vendor sets his crate at a four-way stop,
on the yellow lines in the middle of the street,
his radio low, commenting on the weather, saying to anyone
who will listen, *It's the first day of fall, but warm yet.*

The Sun's Journey Across the Sky

At the top of the hour the minute hand points up,
yet somehow something is still leaning, off-kilter.
Oo'ááł: the sun makes its journey across the sky.
Some days it is on our side, making us lucky.
On others it recedes from us, *nihits'áájí*.
Some call this *unlucky*, but it depends on point of view,
how luck and fortune color your life.

In Oaxaca, color blooms on every wall, every fresco,
on houses and restaurants, in the tassels on women's clothing,
the belts men wear, the food and sauces,
the green mountains in late winter.
Oaxaca, the most comfortably Indian place
I visited during my winter in Mexico.

The skunk was killed trying to cross the street.
It lies sprawled on the pavement as though napping
on grass, trying to cool its belly on a hot day.
Gólízhii biisxí we might say, but I'm unsure
if the verb, *to kill him*, applies to an animal.
*They killed him by sending him to awáalya
(prison) for life*, is the proper usage.
They executed him after sixteen years on death row
is how it was done recently, to a Navajo man, in real life.

As the winter went on, I grew close to my Americans,
sharing inside jokes about hand sanitizer and toilet paper
receptacles, our awkwardness away from American life.
The citizens we walked among looked like me, and I, them.
One day early on, I rode the entire bus route
back to the station, by then the only passenger,
having missed my stop, too embarrassed to ask
where we were in my stumbling Spanish.

We were black, white, Indian, Egyptian,
from the outer boroughs of New York City—
American college kids, looking for an experience,
getting one we'd never bargained for.

The first half of the clock to thirty is counted up—
this many black dots, *dah alzhin*, have passed.
The second half measured by the coming hour—
this many minutes *yidziih* until we arrive at nine,
at the coastal town of Puerto Escondido
to stay a while, to play on the beaches, run screaming
from the swarms of mosquitos so thick they are clouds,
to ride a motorboat along the coast—the expansive Pacific
on one side, an impossibly thick jungle, *la selva*, on the other.

Then begins the last leg of our journey,
the last quarter until colonial Puebla
at the top of the hour, thinking only
of the strain with which we translate in our minds,
unaware that one month *yidziih* of our stay.
That, for some, as in *awáalya*, the *dah alzhin*
are years and there are only fifteen left to go.

Autumn in New England

The trees turned from green to yellow, amber, red,
then splashed their paints on the ground,
the quiet streets covered in quilts of sunset
in the late mornings when breath clouds began to fade
and the sweat from a flag football game
began to dry, allowing one the chill of change.
Something in the way light fell on the hills
and the jackets coming out, formalizing
our education, the daily hike to the brick library,
marked a change outside that mirrored
the one happening within.

I wonder how to describe the border on a weaving,
the alternating black and white, the repeating whorls
that surround the central design of a stylized diamond—
or is it a star? Stars. The introduction of dark red,
the depth a third color creates, rendering
our own bodies three-dimensional.

One day you will wake and the periphery
of your vision will be stitched together and whole,
no longer wavering, lagging behind your central focus,
making you sluggish, weary with the constant effort.
The highway will be clearly visible,
the sound-swallowing fog of a fall day
lifted, warmed by the sun and blown away.

Shield

The air turns cold, the leaves gold and fall.
Change, the one constant.
Package delivery men wear sweaters with their shorts;
a car battery, *chidí bijéí*—its heart—dies and must be replaced.
A couple argues and slams car doors in the night,
knowing they will return later this season or the next,
but this time the break is final.

Poverty whistles through our homes,
tearing papers from desktops,
leaving rice strewn on counters.
Hunger breathes its stale-sour breath
down the backs of our necks.

One must fight them with the stirring sticks:
greasewood branches stripped of their thorns.
Shá bik'ehgo is the sun-wise motion that brings
peace of mind, an ordering of thought
through the blue corn mush, each meal
becoming a wish, intention, prayer—
this, then, is your shield.

For men it is the literal: *k'eet'oh*
worn on the left wrist, also the bow, the quiver
of smoothed and straightened arrows
with which to bring down the enemy,
protect the self, the loved one, shield
the vulnerable flesh, the head, the internal organs.

And in these days we fight, also, the unseen,
grapple with enemies of the mind, harborers of ill-will
either projected upon us or seeded maliciously within—
but your will is brittle as an excavated pot
lined with a network of cracks.

They will knock you down, says the teammate
in your face at halftime, spit spraying his beard
and your cheeks, jabbing his finger into your chest

while the rest of the room remains silent,
watching the ceremony play out,

for there is drama, an unknown ending,
nothing certain in these times, no layup or slam-dunk
can be counted until it licks the net—
Who will return to the court?
What will be your demeanor when *yah aninááh*,
you enter the ringed arena?

Sacred Mountains

The Sherpa is survived by his daughter,
two sons, eight grandchildren. He is predeceased
by his wife, and a son who died after a Himalayan expedition.
He preferred climbing the sacred mountains
without supplemental oxygen,
even as he carried bottles for other mountaineers,
and perhaps this led to the ailments that killed him.

Simple tutorials can be gathered online—
how to replace a car battery, shear sheep.
Even, or perhaps especially, in this disconnected,
connected world, the family gathering takes on new gravity
as we teach ourselves to grow out of helplessness in the face of loss—
lost loved ones, medicine people, those
who kept knowledge, who went out to seek it for us—
and grow new capillaries in our quest for endurance.

Where before there was the void of uncertainty,
the ceiling of pain, now we see, albeit veiled,
a path to understanding the hidden language,
the unspoken names laced into the loom of history.

The moon is nearing full: *K'adée názbas*, they say.
Dear Setting Sun, dear Night,
take with you the plaguing thoughts of day.
Leave me renewed when a new sun rises.

Aak'ee / Fall

Wreathed in fog, leaping out of summer
over the Sangre de Cristos and straight into winter,
autumn surprised us, bringing freezing air and snow.
Northwards, in the Grand Tetons there was proper snow,
billows of it blowing sideways, surprising the experienced hikers
even after the ranger had warned them earlier that day
under a sunny sky. By evening the sky was black with snow
and a pine had fallen onto the hood of their SUV.

A day later we heard the story:
Experienced rock climbers were on the butte face
when a rock fall tore their anchor from the cliff.
An Asian American woman fell some fifty feet, clipped a ledge,
then fell another hundred to the base.
The others nearly fell as well, but being further from the anchor
had time to hang on. They found a faint pulse, and the friends,
then medics performed CPR until the helicopter arrived.
But she did not survive.

On their way back from the last hike that day,
after seeing the ranger, the hikers had seen the helicopter,
the medics pumping someone's chest, and, hearts dropping,
feared the worst for their friends.
But they didn't know these climbers,
and like you and me, only shared the lament
of a good life cut short, albeit more closely,
being of the same profession, understanding the dangers
as well as the immeasurable rewards.

Because she had been a biologist, a PhD, a leader
among the outdoor-enthused, by all accounts bursting
with the ambitious energy we ascribe to a vibrant life.
A door, an invitation to those brown-skinned living,
or wishing to live the adventuring life in America
outdoors among the bright sky, the coarse grasses, the heights,
the sheer gray faces, the solid, unforgiving rock.

We who can picture the dark-haired mother and father,
the brothers and sister who got the phone call,
and, rent from time itself, began the journey to retrieve
their beloved one from that rugged, awful place.

The Warning

Facing the sunset we say *k'adée e'e'aah*,
almost the solid sun has descended beyond our sight—
the word for *west*. An orange haze hangs around the edges
of the far mountains, casting about for some giant greasewood
bush that it can grasp and pull, snapping its thick roots—

The houses attempt to climb the mountainside.
The Red-shafted Flickers flit from piñon tree to tree,
ever higher. The piñons themselves are dropping now;
the cones have opened and birds and small mammals
are feasting, gathering the nuts for their winter caches.
A note taped to the sign says there's a bear on these trails
near sunset, twice noted, so beware you don't disturb him.

Many miles away, in mountains not entirely different
from these, ponderosas are more abundant,
though there are many piñons, too.
There, a man and his aunt have shot a horse
and dragged its carcass to their neighbor's doorstep.
They leave it there. They are all of the same first clan,
but the land dispute of five generations has festered
and the usurpers have borne a family
unafraid of violence, in fact, intent on it,
and the white man the neighbor woman married
was the last straw.

Perhaps it is because she was a pageant-winner
in her time and married this man of means
that they envy her so. Their jealousy fulminates
until they threaten to kill the white husband
if the family continues to summer in these woods,
in their two-room cabin.

This is the way we find the cabin—in disrepair,
the door hinges rusted, the *tóshjeeh* water barrel
rusted as well, the windows boarded, the woods
growing around it, the pine needle bed rising
to cover the porch. The ponderosas still lean
and creak their rhythm, steady over all.

The horse bones are long gone, picked clean,
carried off, scattered to the many directions.
But I believe the story, know it to be true.
A reminder of peril in the world,
of the way the years can twist and warp,
and, also, that first impressions, omens,
are often borne out to be farsighted, true.

North / Náhookos

The earth orbits its angle from fall to winter
to spring, the sun giving us cold and solstice
and equinox. The sun rises and sets,
the south gets its name—
shádi'ááh, *the sun starts to be carried.*

Autumn steps back into late summer,
burning off cold by midmorning,
turning hot as the sun passes not quite overhead,
already on its tilt but singeing us,
the heat more intense for its contrast
with every past autumn, our rains
having been scant and sporadic,
not weeks of afternoon monsoon.

Our oldest grandfather has gone.
Who understands the rites of death?
The observances, the proper distances from event,
from relatives, from those who are closest.
The days that pass, must pass before completion.

Paseo de Peralta goes round and around,
encircling the Plaza, baffling, ensnaring tourists,
defying orderly grid-based municipal design.
The unfinished columns of the Cathedral
stare west down San Francisco Street,
a pair of stately men with their hats blown off,
but who are too proud to retrieve them.

Tourists are scattered on the plaza benches,
timid, exposed, bending surreptitiously to their lunches.
Arab shopkeepers pull their masks down to smoke.
Missing are the Native artists from the Portál
at the Palace of the Governors,
their individual spaces marked by white numbers,
the stencil gaps visible with no blanket to cover them,
no array of pottery, beaded bolos and hatbands,
no silver bracelets and buckles glittering in the sun.

If you fold the mid three fingers to your palm
and raise your hand to the night sky,
you can mark the distance from Big Dipper
to North Star. Next to them is the Little Dipper.
And beyond that, Tsits'aa', the Bowl.
They rotate around the North Star.
Náhookos, the name for north,
wheeling, pivoting around.

On earth we are rotating, spinning
around the axis, arcing around the sun,
marking the passage in length of days,
seasons, warmth, cold, high and low-traveling sun.
Easy. Withhold yourself from hot-blooded imbalance,
for earth revolves again, to a familiar angle of the sun.

Why It's Like This

Behind the black-out curtains as grey dawn light,
hayíiłká, peeks through the window-tops, you wake,
sit up and rub your fascia as though you've been walking
on hard, smooth floors all through the night,
still dreaming the off-kilter dreams of *yikáít'áahjį'*,
limen after deep slumber but before full waking,
when the world dips its gourd into psyche's water.

It's four o'clock, an hour before first cock crows
and wakes the second with the thinner, reedier voice.
One must be unafraid to ask: *Ha'át'íísh biniinaa kót'é?*
Why is it like this? Each time you'll receive
a different answer and within each, kernels reside.

The sour, decaying smell of the expansive chamisa,
its ends pollen-tipped—
Trucks ignite their diesel engines
and gather momentum, loathe to slow for crossers.
The newspaper peddler, a stoic witness behind his hat
and dark sunglasses, raises a hand to the familiar.

Middle day and the neighbor's geese inaugurate a ruckus,
followed by hen and rooster, turkey and dogs;
the three-legged cat hops her way down the block,
antagonizing her rivals.

Midafternoon gives way to late, the sun leans landward,
workers jam the streets, eager to make the commute ordinary again,
to forget the low buzz that twines with air regenerators,
a counter ticking at rear-mind in offices, parlors, tiendas
all the work-long day.

The streets say, *Easy*. The paths say, *Calm*.
The trees sway contentedly in the breeze.
And rabbits worry, though raptors, though owls,
have long been away.

Handmade

You spent all that was given to you
at the maturation ceremony—
burned through the new blankets,
jewelry, flour, and goodwill,
alleging that material must be employed,
consumed, sanded until sparking metal is uncovered,
and only then tossed into the mounded midden.

Rich with clutter and profusion—
cast ring abandoned, shank unsoldered,
wood and porcelain still bearing the bakedwhite stains of corrosive chemicals,
the ghost of your own sweat and chimera—
the work bench had ceased being necessary.

Yet you are grateful for the sketchbooks,
for the bracelets and oxidized belts
behind museum glass, the stones still bright,
their makers' faces captured in black and white—
in which we find inspiration for the tangible,
for the endeavored, the hand-rendered thing.

From our mountain's vantage a new winter
unfurls its frosted cloak—you understand
the revolution of winters counting our age,
witnessing the darker months

in order to paint our world with language,
to give it color, a maze of drama, life.

At the yellow corn close of day
we pull darkness over our bare shoulders,
wrapping ourselves in night.

The Killing Grass

Frost flaking its sap, the gum a streaked and frozen pane
in this blue-lighted dawn, a piñon cone opening.
Chipper, white-headed birds light for morsels,
spiraling up and around trunks and branches,
one looking out for another.

Ripener leans down her face
and touches the tops of these trees.
Despite the dry summer the crop is bountiful
through the ending of Ripener moon.
Families park their cars and trucks beside the highway
along the twisting mountain road to pick and gather—

Sorrow leans against the door, breathing conspicuously
like someone with an audience,
waiting for the inevitable turn of a knob, the welcome in.
The aggressors are relentless, tending trash
to feed their flames, welcoming the acrid smell,
the hard smoke, so one must keep hold of the day,
mark its passing by the proper colors:
first, blue expanse, then a yellow-orange journey
to horizon and, finally, night's fire-lit music,
day's quiet hinge.

One must not forget the animals,
created holy as well, whose care comforts and calms.
As my grandmother says, I recommend it,
it keeps you going, makes you get up and do things—
whether cat or dog, bird or head of sheep
who rely on you for water, love, sustenance,
whom you must protect from dangers,
from *ch'il aghání* that looks like green grass,
but is The Plant That Kills—
for their health is yours.

University

The boy leapt onto the grass and metal sculpture
and crowed, a bird proclaiming vitality, strength,
brandishing his comb, flexing in the lamp-starred night.
His first brush with love, first dive to its depths,
living in another's room, unabashed of the uneven count—
three in a room overspilling the pair of beds.

Autumn was alive with fire. She teased
and he hugged her to him, making the donut shop
attendants break into smile in spite of themselves,
desperate as they were to match the gray sky
even as the maples caught fire along the streets outside.

That time when, amplified perhaps by a boreal campus,
the skies and mind are wide, our futures prosper,
emblazoned with accomplishment, skin is smooth,
and we thrill to newfound contours
of muscle and sinew, a sloping abdomen.

Even as the days declined and night began
to lower its ceiling they desired more and more,
touching some limit, troubled here and there
by shouts and tears as ambitions clashed,
schedules overrode and other stars, too,
began to shine through the curtain.

They could have learned the import of ending then,
the need for descent and denouement,
change and the ever-spinning earth,
but it was difficult to understand, even confronted
with its constant formulas in thick-sheafed books,
on glaring whiteboards—

And like so many lovers, when met with the disintegration
of their careful world, they tore holes in each other,
injured each other, their endeavors undressed,
coupled dreams now brittle and unstable
like the opaque, streaked sheet of ice over a pond
not yet solid enough to bear the weight of a foot.

Theirs ended in fire, a supernova visible,
as they thought then, for all the world to see.
They still remember that flash, though it's smaller now,
compacted within their hearts, fused with so many others.
But the grain is still visible
if you stoop and look closely.

Nomenclature

From the way it hangs there—heavy or askew,
light or energetic—the moon can tell you
what the month will be, where its sinkholes lie,
the tenor of your harvest.

Life goes on. We call our relatives into our computers,
wait for their reply, walk the mall, patronize
the immigrant masseuse, the *whap-whap* papery now
in rubber-gloved hands.

The barbers and stylists have returned—
idle though, between cuts, having swept
beneath all the chairs and double-checked the register;
the new ropes course towers bright and lonely in the atrium.

I never knew that the place names where I'm from
refer to one river, its source underground, its carving
path through Canyon de Chelly and finally to exit—

I'd thought the water named *Tséhílí*,
Tódzís'á, Ch'ínlí, was each its own separate spring or pond,
not understanding the web of water, the inherent gravity

and careful design of our nomenclature
and once again I am opened, a map whose borders
are expanded by a flashlight.

Out here the stars are visible but barely,
the brightest ones are likely planets;
walking as a pair, we teach each other their names,
imagining what we can't remember.

Creation Story

To turn a page, to break the crust of fresh snow
underfoot on the mountaintop, the wind turning,
cleaving the old world even as a hurricane
bears down on a city too close to the shore,
heedless of the example of the ancients—
wind that gives life, but if unheeded,
will take it, too.

To release your grip on the nylon cable
that you'd been clutching all this time,
fearful of the drop. After coming this far,
perhaps more fearful of the loss of all those hours,
that work in climbing this high,
the scraped knuckles, raw fingers, bruised toes.
Now muscle and sinew tremors with the strain
to hold yourself in place, suspended,
for the anchors above have been severed
by falling rock and the spotter below
has vanished with oncoming night.

To study a religious book every morning,
pouring the self into it, attempting a sieve
of the mind, the soul, accomplishing a broadening,
a deepening, and a capacity for commerce
and farsightedness as a past takes shape,
full of deeds and wonder.

To make use of a car, of a horse,
of a shoe; to make use of a word, a language,
of one's hands to harvest the thorny boughs,
then shuck them, scrape them, make them smooth,
assemble by length, tie in a bundle;
to make this most useful and ready instrument
to repel hunger, reject poverty,
call down rain and bounty.

To awake to trees and the birds within them,
to climb steep mountain trails, cautious of a bear
sighted yesterday in each startled wing flutter,
cracked stem in the undergrowth, movement
at vision's periphery, relearning fear,
the prickle at the ears and neck, even as sun descends
to setting, blasting your face with rays.

A Wedding

An update is needed to bring *naaki yáál*, two bits,
to a quarter, four bits, *díí yáál*, to fifty cents—
but we have leapt over that period of the treaty
and straight into a deepening void,
crossing the event horizon, the lip of exponential

gravity, and I am in awe of my sister the mathematician,
with whom I was born running,
who builds upon a vast latticework, a mechanic
who cycles through her knowledge of engine, carb,

transmission, battery, electrical wiring, and finds
some sense of equilibrium, a symmetry
in the imbalance. Immaterial then,
to step backwards in bridging the languages' gap,
the gulf superficial, ultimately, in nature.

The moon retreats from halfway, descends
the frosted slopes, grazes the crackling sap
and brittle pinecones, rattles the shells
that remained hollow but for the desiccated
oval coins that never became meat.

The shade house boughs are dry now and crackling,
but at the wedding they were green
and full, and oversaw the meeting we made,
the gathering of disparate families,
of cultures worlds apart.

I peer under the floorboards where the dog
stows her pups; I split open the Ponderosa stump
to find creamy grubs, sluggish in the cold,
shocking in their flavor: sweet, resembling
the pine's fragrant bark and its cousin's brawny fruit.

I kneel there, a pleasing dolor among the dirt
and woodchips, and view the wedding from the other side—
all the people arrayed before my brother and his wife,
while many more are on tiptoe, looking in.

Dididoołjah

To emerge, an awful fire held aloft—

To ignore the metal's chiming, the bell's gonging,
to drink in the bitter herbs and hold them down,
to master the body, traverse the ridge, sink
into the dark, steaming heat when internal air
gains equilibrium without, to hold the balance
past the first gasp, the second and third weakness
and on into waking dream, the organ view,
the liquid stream through heart to stomach to intestine—

To sweat rivering down the temple, the chest
and abdomen, the very hair on the shin,
reveling in the comparative cool of the earth—

This, then, is shield, is armor, cloak, and air,
the routine of constancy, the revolution,
ever evolving sun, more, nááná, *again* its rays
on your face, this time cooler, mark its progress
and your mapped point within that arc,
your small coordinates, bright and slowly moving—

The heavy oak branch finally cracks and splinters
and thuds to earth, the Ponderosa leans to its mate,
the natural grasses reclaim the field.
One-That-Sticks takes over, spreads its green hands—
New cars park beside the old hulk,
new voices grown rougher and deeper resound within—
The city walking trail up the mountain
littered with newly unearthed debris—

This is where the muscles tense and fire
when we have learned finally to respect the fall,
review the crash, to honor its teachings
as you would those of a master—
hanging on every word, photographing with the mind.

For the image is precious, gravity lives there,
the future sends its wind with the snap of a blanket,
the past has awakened, throwing water on your face,
imploring you to rise, scrape your crusted eyes,
gather fuel, *make a fire.*

A Speech

In the age of evolution we strove.
Traveling, we saw the ocean roiled

and roiling, there found a new
inheritance, renewed by water,

flesh, and blood. Welcoming our clan's
solid founding, we knew it even then:

Everyone needs water, finds its uses.
To speak directly, without intermediary

in your call for winter, for cold
and snow, for your horses' wintering,

and your sheep's watering, for our wholesome
return from traveling.

For the path is on many axes—
time, space, and spirit, realized with words

shared as if they were berries,
piñons picked in contrast to one's loose

and flying hair that incurs scolds
from those with standing.

Therefore praise your cattle's health,
may they live in water, food, and multiply,

grow until their backbones crowd
this mountainous valley,

hip to shoulder parallel—
The way you spoke, turning left and right,

invoking Gods, and the ones to come
who you could not see.

Swifts and Swallows

Atop the angled mountain, the high, tilted ridge,
swifts and swallows wheel at the shear—
their small feet tucked, the swifts mating in air.

Spruce trundle upwards from the green litter,
their cones recognized by the three-pronged bracts;
fir grow alongside them, spreading their branches

as we splay fingers for balance, for sense in the dark.
Today the wind blows hard up the rock face,
pushes us back when we approach the edge

to look out upon the shattered city arrayed below.
Tsoodził, South Mountain, just visible in the distant haze.
The firs have flattened needles with rounded tips;

the spruces' are square with sharp tips.
In these harsh gales tourists lean, wrap thin jackets
about their shoulders, tighten hoods about faces.

Hardship is a human right, cold air in the lungs
a necessary invigoration, a strong, sinewy grip
about water and bone, our deceptively fragile bodies—

The test, the beings' exam discernable,
the deadfall, undergrowth, and fungus all of a piece,
light green lichen hangs from the Corkbark Fir—

Now the wind is new, it becomes a bellow.
To reach the mountain we'd driven through a brown and windy basin,
an old shady pueblo, the turquoise mine long closed,

past the torn-up earth where trucks
repaired the towering transformers and electrical lines and turned—
the flashing roofs of houses foreshadowing

a smaller scale of the view to come,
the houses growing thicker nearer the mountain,
American flags staked and whipping in the wind.

Now we descend to the base,
encounter a snarl of traffic, flashing lights,
a uniformed man photographing evidence

of the car, frozen where it had been gaining
the highway from the gas station, its family huddled under a tree.
The motorcycle still leans against the dented door

like a horse trying to force its way through.
The swifts dart and dive, long gone from the ridge
on their journey to Central, then South America

to light in the distant, blue-broken dawn.

Counting

Omen's breathy wings, distant shouts,
memory divided into shelves and boxes,
beads scattered across the floor,
here glass, here shell, turquoise, fluted silver,
jet, and a spongy apple coral—

A child's cheek dimple gradually subsumed
by the map of time, birth, marriage, career, and family.
To be overly stimulated, joints rattling
at every police siren and flash,
every mailman's boot, every journalist's brittle morality.
The laminated seal has begun to peel—

A man has chained himself to a wire barrier,
the construction trucks continue to reverse,
the cranes to crane and hoist unsettled earth.
He paints his own face on the barrier,
lingers overlong, suffers broken bones
he'd not counted on—

The syllables of counting are spread unevenly,
making breathing difficult even in the mind.
Brandishing blue gloves, the doctor examines,
sunrays descend upon the crooked valley
like a figure tipped too far, falling truly,
sweeping all in his crash—

The singer pulls his hand back,
having seen something he'd rather forget,
debates whether to give the full diagnosis,
the soul's wounded shriek.
Work has begun, the food laid before us
in enameled dishes rich with energy,
glistening of wealth.

Warlike

Male constellation and female constellation
revolve around the North Star, never touching,
never running away, a family around a fire,
tending, imparting the home with the smell
of cooking and wind-swept clothes, of sweat.

With the arrival of metal hats and breastplates
came the harrowing of orchards and songs,
of fully-ripened ceremony, of metaphor, afternoon yellows,
of striving beyond sight to the edges of the universe,
of the collective climb to inmost achievement.

Lacking other enemies, seeking travail and anguish,
to birth war among ourselves.
A grand, studied phenomena renewed now at scale,
in our new and warlike form.
The mountains rise above us waiting to be called upon,
and, knowledge regained, to be questioned again—
is it not so?

The knitted and contracted face we present
is a surface condition, our bodies green and supple with sap,
needing insistent hands, strong fingers to encourage a new molding,
to brush away the waxen flakes and unfold until
a person stands there—tall, competent,
facing the awakening east.

Neighborhood

Dogs chase the kids—two boys and a girl on bikes
down the street and overtake the boy who is on foot.

In the bare spot where a trailer used to be,
two Chinese elms lean over the absent roof,

no longer scraping walls and windows,
while pipes and plugs gape like dry, severed veins.

A game of football in the neighborhood's last
undeveloped clearing: the quarterback draws up the play

with his finger in the dirt, X's and slants,
shielding it from their adversaries,

teammates nodding even when they don't understand,
just happy to share a secret. *Ready, BREAK—*

The deepest snowfall in thirty years and they come together
to build snowmen, angels, forts, start snow fights—

boys and girls on the cusp of an uneven footing,
the last time they will all be so free together.

The distant lights of a big-tent revival—
dust spirals upward in flurries.

Summer sun sets among the mittened buttes.
Lightning strikes and every child kneels

before the bowl on the classroom's carpeted floor,
then must extend to their bellies to drink the water—

bitter, bodied with herbs—
protection from the lightning's power.

Glancing at each other, eyeing
the medicine man in headband and blazer,

whispering until they are scolded in this incongruous setting.
New houses rise and replace the trailers

with a more congruous order, the interiors smelling of fresh
caulking and paint. When tentatively the levers are pressed,

impossibly, throatily, magically among the fresh, red dirt,
the expansive westward view, the toilets flush.

Work

I was conscripted
by the wind's unceasing lean
the stars' unclouded whirl
apricots green yet and tough
my mind similarly sugarless.
By the mountains' frosted sweep
skewered as a wild biting dog
on the end of a spear
those fallen fruits are
feasts for ants and wasps
the industrious sweepers
of the ground building the world
whole again setting example
of the potential of congruous work.
But conscription can be fought
the summons refused and dodged
hidden from in some cave
ignoring the wind's howling.
Earth is patient with the humans
and will outwait us
the incandescent spikes in our blood.
So I was flushed out
and joined the ranks of workmen
of trainees stumbling into day
set roughly in our uniforms
brought before our labor.
Your turn is now.
Quit that backward lean.
The dawn has turned
from middle morning in truth
nearer middle day.
The sun shines on your head
muscles gird your skeleton
sweat is made also for measurement
for another to kiss and lick
to find your own satisfaction
to dry, encrust and give you an earned smell.

Adolescence

When the young piñon grows green, when the buds
of its green cones glisten with sap, the heat haze rises,

the exhaust-fog breaks apart, our prayer is heard, our goals
solidified—new car, new job, new government compromise—

releasing you from your choke of tasks, your mountain of busywork.
Sovereignty survives the midnight break-in, the friends' betrayal

at a post-festival dinner party, and the Council meeting
has been called to order, introductions made, clans recited.

Now the real business—shields raised, keyboards brandished,
pretense shucked from fibrous, reedy voices ready to speech-make,

dress the undermining comment in a story of praise.
The boarding school has been boarded up, the surviving buildings

converted into a clinic. The language remains English, and—caregiving
grown expensive—our aunts, our little mothers quarrel,

ceremonies come undone, a sheep bleats in the pickup bed,
hog-tied, bloating, waiting in vain to be slaughtered.

We wait for stores to reopen, repost their sale signs so we can careen
once more through the aisles. The National Guard patrols

the supermarket's automatic doors with assault rifles,
transients reuse the disposables, Great Aunt awaits a call

on the split computer screen. Call on the offering, raise your material,
pinched between thumb and forefinger, in a humble, unpresuming,

unassuming way for the young piñon to see, and remember the chewy,
clinging texture, the sap's bitter-mint taste.

Idiom

The act of speaking has been completed: hojoolne'—
not necessarily in the past as on a timeline

but that one has finished speaking, talking, telling,
the action is completed—hold that in your mind.

From whom did you learn the ceremony? In this case
learned is the completion, to have it in your repertoire,

your bank of learning. I walked the jewelry store yesterday,
peering through the glass at all that wealth,

the wealth of ages—squash blossoms, bolo ties, concho belts
on the wall. The fiddle player plays on the plaza, face hidden

under her wide-brimmed hat, bending with the melody,
so full of energy, calves muscular from a life dancing in place.

We must use the language every day—Háágóósh díníyá?
Where are you off to? Naanishgóó déyá. I'm off to work.

For in the quotidian we find the gradual change, the evolution
of life, slow, imperceptible aging, new technologies,

computers, phones, whole worlds living in the man-made
electrical ether and there must be names for them—

wind-lives-within-it, speaks from it, relays messages through it.
Language shifts to accommodate the needs and wants of life,

becomes imperiled when our lives have moved so far beyond
the original mindset, have outstripped and sped down

a material path we are loathe to go with our language,
sensing instinctively its rocky shallows even as we speed

along its surface, enamored with the blurring ripples below,
as a roadrunner is enraptured by another roadrunner—

its comb rising, strikingly red and orange—
behind the window, who, impossibly,

also holds a striped lizard in its beak.
The wind had made us, given us life,

breathing out through the whorls at our fingertips;
water fills us and slakes our thirst, moistening

the mud of our material as fire sparks and lights the mind.
Is it really so hard to believe that we lift language,

rub our bodies with it, wrap it about our ribs,
iron it into our headbands, fold them carefully,

and tie them about our heads? We are, after all,
those who collaborate, raising logs into homes and hogans,

and this effort is not completed, is k'ad, imperfect,
in fact, continually imperfect, and we will remain

in the act of doing, speaking, thinking, iteratively
composing and breaking down, inventing now a new dialect.

About the Author

Chee Brossy is a poet and fiction writer. He was born in Chinle, Arizona, and raised in Red Mesa, Arizona, in the Navajo Nation. He is the author of the poetry books *Burntwater* and *The Strings Are Lightning and Hold You In* and the novella *Fighters*. His writing has appeared in *Denver Quarterly, Kenyon Review, PRISM International, Southern Indiana Review*, and elsewhere. He has been a fellow at the Vermont Studio Center. He is Navajo of the Water Flows Together clan and lives in New Mexico.

About The Word Works

Since its founding in 1974, The Word Works has steadily published volumes of contemporary poetry and presented public programs. Its imprints include The Washington Prize, The Tenth Gate Prize, The Hilary Tham Capital Collection, and International Editions. There is also an open reading period in May and June.

Monthly, The Word Works offers free programs in its Café Muse Literary Salon. Starting in 2023, the winners of the Jacklyn Potter Young Poets Competition will be presented in the June Café Muse program.

As a 501(c)3 organization, The Word Works has received awards from the National Endowment for the Arts, the National Endowment for the Humanities, the D.C. Commission on the Arts & Humanities, the Witter Bynner Foundation, Poets & Writers, The Writer's Center, Bell Atlantic, the David G. Taft Foundation, and others, including many generous private patrons.

An archive of artistic and administrative materials in the Washington Writing Archive is housed in the George Washington University Gelman Library. The Word Works is a member of the Community of Literary Magazines and Presses and its books are distributed by Small Press Distribution.

wordworksbooks.org

Winners of the Washington Prize

Nathalie Anderson, *Following Fred Astaire*, 1998
Michael Atkinson, *One Hundred Children Waiting for a Train*, 2001
Molly Bashaw, *The Whole Field Still Moving Inside It*, 2013
Carrie Bennett, *biography of water*, 2004
Peter Blair, *Last Heat*, 1999
John Bradley, *Love-in-Idleness: The Poetry of Roberto Zingarello*, 1989, 2ND edition 2014
Christopher Bursk, *The Way Water Rubs Stone*, 1988
Richard Carr, *Ace*, 2008
Jamison Crabtree, *Rel[AM]ent*, 2014
Jessica Cuello, *Hunt*, 2016
Barbara Duffey, *Simple Machines*, 2015
B. K. Fischer, *St. Rage's Vault*, 2012
Linda Lee Harper, *Toward Desire*, 1995
Ann Rae Jonas, *A Diamond Is Hard but Not Tough*, 1997
Meg Kearney, *All Morning the Crows*, 2020
Annie Kim, *Eros, Unbroken*, 2019
Susan Lewis, *Zoom*, 2017
Frannie Lindsay, *Mayweed*, 2009
Richard Lyons, *Fleur Carnivore*, 2005
Elaine Magarrell, *Blameless Lives*, 1991
Fred Marchant, *Tipping Point*, 1993, 2ND edition 2013
Radha Marcum, *Pine Soot Tendon Bone*, 2023
Nils Michals, *Gembox*, 2018
Ron Mohring, *Survivable World*, 2003
Barbara Moore, *Farewell to the Body*, 1990
Naomi Mulvihill, *The Knife Thrower's Girl*, 2022
Brad Richard, *Motion Studies*, 2010
Jay Rogoff, *The Cutoff*, 1994
Prartho Sereno, *Call From Paris*, 2007, 2ND edition 2013
Enid Shomer, *Stalking the Florida Panther*, 1987
John Surowiecki, *The Hat City After Men Stopped Wearing Hats*, 2006
Sharon Suzuki-Martinez, *The Loneliest Whale Blues*, 2021
Miles Waggener, *Phoenix Suites*, 2002
Charlotte Warren, *Gandhi's Lap*, 2000
Mike White, *How to Make a Bird With Two Hands*, 2011
Nancy White, *Sun, Moon, Salt*, 1992, 2ND edition 2010
George Young, *Spinoza's Mouse*, 1996

www.ingramcontent.com/pod-product-compliance
Lightning Source LLC
Chambersburg PA
CBHW032010080426
42735CB00007B/558